POETICA 11

Old English Riddles

Poetica is a series of texts, translations and miscellan-
eous works relating to poetry. The purpose of the
series is to provide a library of important works from
all ages and cultures.

Editor: Peter Jay
Advisory editors: Michael Hamburger,
Peter Levi, Peter Whigham
and Betty Radice

Eliza Wheatn
Jan 05

BY MICHAEL ALEXANDER

poetry

Twelve Poems, 1978

translations

The Earliest English Poems, 1966
Beowulf, 1973

criticism

The Poetic Achievement of Ezra Pound, 1979
The Prologue to the Canterbury Tales, 1980
The Knight's Tale, 1981
A History of Old English Literature, 1983

Michael Alexander

Old English Riddles

from the Exeter Book

Anvil Press Poetry

Published in 1980
by Anvil Press Poetry
69 King George Street London SE10 8PX
85646 070 2

Reprinted with corrections in 1982
Reprinted 1984

This book has been published
with financial assistance from
The Arts Council of Great Britain

Printed in England by
Skelton's Press Ltd, Wellingborough

to Felicity Riddy

The translator acknowledges assistance from the Arts Council of Great Britain.

Acknowledgement is also due to W. S. Mackie and the Oxford University Press for the extracts from *The Exeter Book* (Early English Text Society) in Riddle 92; and to D. C. Heath for the quotations from Wyatt's *Old English Riddles;* also to the Editor of *Agenda* in whose pages some of these translations first appeared.

Preface

THE OLD ENGLISH RIDDLES survive through the Exeter Book, a manuscript of about the year 1000, left to Exeter Cathedral by its first bishop, Leofric, who died in 1072. The Exeter Book is a verse miscellany, including *The Wanderer* and *The Seafarer* and several of the more famous short poems in Old English. The riddles—there are over ninety in the manuscript—have intrigued scholars and translators since Hickes in 1703, and interest has increased in recent years. Translators are drawn not only by the appealing brevity of the riddle—most of them are, like poems in modern anthologies, less than a page in length—but by the concision and play of language that often accompany this brevity. The riddles are also attractive to readers with any curiosity: unlike most Old English poetry, they are frequently neither heroic nor improving. Dr Johnson would have found many of them low and mean—but they are also innocent and disarming. The solution is usually a familiar object of the house, hall, farmyard, monastery or battlefield, or else something in nature—an animal, bird, plant or some feature of the elements. There is often charm as well as an anthropological interest in the domestic riddles, and in the natural ones an inwardness that we have lost. But the essence of the riddles is enigma. Something speaks to us from twelve hundred years ago, directly, however mysteriously, and, in the first person, asks us to guess its name.

This selection includes fifty-four of these Exeter riddles. They were probably composed or written down two or three hundred years before the Exeter Book was compiled or copied, and some of them will be older than that, since the riddle is traditional and still flourishes in spoken form in traditional societies. Like other forms with folk origins—charms and spells—the riddle, even in learned later examples, has often kept some primal quality, and even the Christian riddles are animistic by virtue of the habit of mind involved in the form itself. The greatest of

Christian poems in Old English, *The Dream of the Rood,* is in the form of a riddle.

Historically, riddling seems to have been at the peak of its British popularity in the monasteries of Bede's lifetime (673-735), and later. To quote the admirable Wyatt:

> 'The riddles of the Exeter Book form one of several extant collections of enigmas attributed to Englishmen of the seventh and eighth centuries—the Ænigmata ' of Aldhelm (640-709), Bishop of Sherborne, of Tatwine, Archbishop of Canterbury (731-734), of Eusebius (Hwætberht), Abbot of Wearmouth (716-c.747), of Boniface (Winfrith), the Lorsch Riddles, and those attributed to Bede, with those of Alcuin (735-804), Archbishop of York. Prose conversation manuals, such as Ælfric's *Colloquies*, and especially Alcuin's *Disputatio inter Pippinum et Alcuinum,* show a close affinity to these puzzles.
>
> The literary origin, as distinguished from the prevalence of popular riddles, of all these collections is to be found in the Ænigmata of one Symphosius, whether the minor poet Firmianus Symphosius Cælius or not we cannot tell. Some critics place the riddler as early as the 2nd century A.D., others as late as the 6th. There is a prologue of seventeen hexameters, mentioning the poet by name; then come a hundred (or a hundred and one, a cuckoo-riddle being doubtful) three-line hexameter puzzles.'

But only about ten of the Old English riddles seem directly taken from these Latin riddles; another twenty take hints from Aldhelm's *Ænigmata.* German scholars used to stress the derivation from Latin, English scholars to deny it. In any case, the tradition is more than its practitioners. Some of the riddles were translated, some composed, some written down from popular tradition—all, we must presume, by monks. That the hand which held the quill was a monastic hand need surprise only those who presume that monks have none of the interests natural to men. During the period at which these riddles were composed, monasticism and literacy, not to say civilization, were virtually synonymous. The sort of person who reads riddles today would almost certainly have been a member of a regular order in the eighth century. St Benedict, of course, permitted innocent relaxation in his Rule, and the names above in Wyatt's list, which includes three saints, are luminaries of the Anglo-Saxon Church as well of our early literature. Aldhelm and Bede wrote much in the vernacular which has not survived. Wyatt, however, notes of the Latin enigmas of the Archbishop of Canterbury, 'Though Tatwine borrows something from Aldhelm he is not unoriginal, but he is always dull.' He adds, of Bede's abbot, 'Eusebius is, if possible, duller than Tatwine.'

The Exeter riddles are uneven but they are rarely dull. I have adopted the numbering of W. S. Mackie's edition of the Exeter Book for the Early English Text Society, and of his ninety-four riddles, twenty are too inaccessible to be worth translating here; in making this selection, I have set aside another twenty. The inadmissibles are either incomplete because of damage to the manuscript, or unsolved, or involve runic characters; I have included one example of each of these. Of the twenty not chosen, some duplicate other riddles and others are obscure. Twenty of the riddles included previously appeared in *The Earliest English Poems*, and are reproduced by kind permission of Penguin Books Ltd.

The translations are poetic in intention, although they are faithful and as accurate as I could make them while following the Old English versification. I have been more careful to do this in making the thirty-three new translations for this selection originally commissioned by Tony Rudolf, whose Menard Press had previously published Riddle 8 as a postcard. I am grateful to Mr Rudolf for suggesting this book, to the Arts Council of Great Britain for their assistance, and to Peter Jay, who is all a publisher should be. Other scholarly debts and details are recorded in the notes at the back of the book, as are the solutions which have been proposed for the riddles by modern scholars.

MICHAEL ALEXANDER

1

What man so quick and clever of wit
To divine who it is who drives me on my course
When I arise in my strength and sudden fury,
Threatening hugely, throwing myself about,
Bursting across country, burning men's houses
And sacking their dwellings? Dark smoke
Rises above the roofs. Roaring is on the earth,
The sudden death of men. When I move the forest,
The flourishing groves, I fell the trees;
The powers above dispatch me to wander
Far on my range, roofed in with the waters.
I have on my back what buried the forms
Of dwellers on earth deep in ocean,
Body and soul. Say who hides me
Or how I am called who carry these burdens.

2

Sometimes I melt away, when men do not expect it,
Beneath the welter of the waves to visit
The bottom of the sea, the Spearman's floor.
Ocean is aroused, rolls his foam. . .
The whale-pond roars and rages loudly,
The tides beat the shores, and at times cast up
Stones and sand, seaweed and waves
Against the steep cliffs, when, struggling under
The might of the ocean, I make its floor shake,
The vast sea-plains. This vault of water
I may not leave until allowed by the one
Who directs all my ways. Wise man, say now
Who it is that brings me from the embracing ocean
When those currents grow calm again
And the waves that covered me quieten once more.

3

Sometimes my Lord sends me below
The fortunate earth, confines me narrowly
Beneath her broad breast and binds me to remain there,
Pens this mighty power in darkness;
Rudely he cramps me, where the rock sits
Hard on my back. From this hateful place
I have no escape, but I shake the foundation
Of the houses of men. High walls tremble
Above the household; the horn-gabled buildings,
Men's dwellings, quake. All quiet seems
The air above the land, and the ocean sleeps,
Until from my prison I press upwards
According to his prompting who caught me at first
And in the beginning girded on me
The fetters and chains that afford no escape
From the power of the one who points out my ways.

    Sometimes I must whip up the waves from above,
Stir the tides up and steer shoreward
A flint-grey flood. The foamy breaker
Fights the cliff. There climbs above the deep
A hill of hoar water, and, behind it as it comes
Driven by the sea, its dark successor,
So that they match themselves with the mighty headlands
That march with the shore. The ship then is in uproar,
The sea's guests shout. Sheer and unmoving,
The stony heights await the onset of the seas,
As their lofty company crowds into the bay
And shatter on the cliffs. Then the ship must know
A still worse struggle if the sea bears her off,
With her complement of souls, at that season of fear:
She shall be deprived of dominion there,
Her life dashed from her: lathered she rides
The backs of the waves. The worst terror then

Is revealed to men, among those I must heed,
Strong in my onset. Who stills this tumult?

  Sometimes I rush through what rides on my back,
The dark moisture-bearers, drive them asunder
With their bellying waters; or bring them once more
Sliding together. The greatest of sounds is it,
The ear-splitting clap of overhead thunder
When one cloud sharply encounters another,
Edge against edge. These umber creatures
Go sweeping over the peoples, sweating flame,
White fire. They forge on above men,
Black thunder-clouds, bellowing loudly,
Ramping and lowering. They allow dark raindrops
To come pattering down, drop from their breast,
Distil from their bellies. Braying onward come
Their terrible troops: disaster stalks
Among mankind, commotion and fear
Spread through the cities, as the spectres stray
And darkly shoot their sharp weapons.
The fool fears not these fatal darts,
Yet if the true Lord allows an arrow,
A tearing shaft from the tumult above,
To streak down straight through the rain,
He dies nevertheless. Not many live
Once the swift foeman's weapon has touched them.
I bring about the beginning of that conflict
When among the clash of clouds I go up
To thrust with power through the thickest of it
Above the cloud tops, where battalions
Deafen the heavens. Then I descend again
Below the cloud-cover close to the land
And, moved once more by my mighty Lord,
Hoist onto my back what I have to carry.

  Thus I, a strong servant, stir wars by turns:
Sometimes under the earth, sometimes under the waves

Descending low; or I disturb the waters
Of ocean from above; or ascending high
I gather the cloud-wrack, career far
In my strength and swiftness. Say what I am called,
Or who arouses me when I must rest no more,
Or when I am still who stays me then.

5

An outsider am I, whom iron has wounded
And swords have scarred; sated with fighting,
Weary of weapons. War I see often,
Cruel conflict: comfort I do not look for,
That succour should come to me in the clash of war
Before I perish completely among men.
What hammers leave, the hard-edged and keen-ground
Handiwork of smiths, smites and shears me
At the wall of the city. I await always
A still worse combat. No kind of doctor
Could I ever find in any settlement
Who could with his herbs heal up these wounds,
But the sword-cuts increase upon me
Day and night from deadly blows.

7

When it is earth I tread, make tracks upon water
Or keep the houses, hushed is my clothing,
Clothing that can hoist me above house-ridges,
At times toss me into the tall heaven
Where the strong cloud-wind carries me on
Over cities and countries; accoutrements that
Throb out sound, thrilling strokes,
Deep-soughing song, as I sail alone
Over field and flood, faring on,
Resting nowhere. My name is ——.

8

I speak through mouth in many voices,
Sing in wrenches, ever I wrestle
Sound in my throat, shout out loudly,
Keep to my custom, curb not my crying,
Old evening singer, I bring in bliss
To the dwelling of men; when with my thrilling
Throat I storm, still they sit
By the hearth, listening.
                    Say what I am,
Who call so clear, a clowning singer,
Loud-mouthed mimic, to men proclaiming
Much that is welcome.

9

Abandoned unborn by my begetters
I was still dead a few spring days ago:
No beat in the breast, no breath in me.

A kinswoman covered me in the clothes she wore,
No kind but kind indeed, I was coddled and swaddled
As close as I had been a baby of her own,
Until, as had been shaped, so shielded, though no kin,
The unguessed guest grew great with life.

She fended for me, fostered me, she fed me up,
Till I was of a size to set my bounds
Further afield. She had fewer dear
Sons and daughters because she did so.

10

My beak was in a narrow place: beneath and by me
Flowed the flood. Far below ocean's
Whelming streams was it that I grew,
Covered by the waves, a wandering spar
Of wood the only near neighbour of my body.
I was full of life when I left the embracing
Wood and water, wore my black.
Among my equipment was much white also
When the air took me and tossed me up living,
The wind from the wave: widely it bore me
Over the seal's bath. Say what I am called.

11

Tawny my raiment, yet red and gleaming
Jewels adorn my dress also.
I send the simple astray and stir the fool
To rash undertakings; others I hold back
From wiser ways. Why in their madness
Of stolen wits and straying courses
They extol my dark dealings to everyone
I have no idea. Dearly shall they pay for this
When the Highest brings forth the best of treasures
If they have not given up this unwise usage.

12

While my ghost lives I go on feet,
Rend the ground, green leas.
When breath is gone I bind the hands
Of swart Welsh; worthier men, too.
I may be a bottle: bold warrior
Swigs from my belly. Or a bride may set
Proudly her foot on me. Or, far from her Wales,
A dark-headed girl grabs and squeezes me,
Silly with drink, and in the dark night
Wets me with water, or warms me up
Before the fire. Fetched between breasts
By her hot hand, while she heaves about
I must stroke her swart part. Say my name:
Who living live off the land's wealth
And, when dead, drudge for men.

14

I was armed at all points. Yet a proud youth
Now binds me with wire, with wound gold and silver,
A young retainer. At times men kiss me.
Sometimes with a sound I summon to battle
Gracious companions; or go on a horse
Over the march. Over the sea sometimes
A sea-stallion bears me, brightly ornate.
Or one of the maidens may, ring-adorned,
Fill my bosom. On the board sometimes
I have to lie stripped, stark and headless.
Sometimes I hang above, handsome on the wall,
Equipped and mounted, where men are drinking.
At times the defenders take me on horseback,
A chief arm of the troop; treasure-adorned,
I must swallow the breath from the bosom of one.
And it is my voice that invites the proud
Warriors to wine; and winds the alarm
That restores what has been wickedly stolen,
Puts foes to flight. Find out my name!

15

My neck is white. Not so my head,
Which is brown, like my sides. I am swift on my feet,
And I bear weapons: bristles on my cheeks,
Bristles on my back. Above my eyes
Two ears steeple. I step on my toes
On the green grass. Grief is my portion
If a certain savage warrior
Finds me at home with my family quietly
Keeping our dwelling. If I dally in the house
With my brood about me when this brutal stranger
Comes to my door, death is their portion.
Timidly must I then take my offspring
To safety by flight, flee our homeland.
If he still comes crawling on his chest
Doggedly after me, I dare not await
His attack in the chamber, a choice to avoid.
Rather I must hastily, with hands and feet
Drive a way through the depths of the hill.
If I can bring my brood outside
Through a hole in the bank, a hidden by-way,
I can easily preserve the precious lives
Of my nearest and dearest. No need for me then
To have the least fear of the fierce hound's attack.
If the cruel foe comes after me
Along the narrow paths, he shall not be disappointed
Of a warlike meeting on his way to battle.
Once I have broken out through the back of the hill
I shall turn with spite the tines I carry
On the hated foes I have fled so long.

16

I have to strive against the sea and struggle with the wind,
Often battle with both. Abandoning homeland,
I go in search of ground under water.
If I stay still I have strength for the fight;
If this fails to happen, their force is the greater:
Tearing at me, they soon turn me in flight.
They wish to plunder what I am employed to guard.
Yet I can stop them, if the strain is taken
By the rocks — and my tail. Tell my name.

18

I have a mouth — I am a marvellous creature —
And a swollen belly; yet before company
As you see, I am silent, cannot speak a word.
I came with many of my kindred in a ship.

25

I'm the world's wonder, for I make women happy:
A boon to the neighbourhood, a bane to no one,
Though I may perhaps prick the one who picks me.

I am set well up, stand in a bed,
Have a roughish root. Rarely (though it happens)
A churl's daughter more daring than the rest—
And lovelier! —lays hold of me,
Rushes my red top, wrenches at my head,
And lays me in the larder. She learns soon enough,
The curly-haired creature who clamps me so,
Of my meeting with her: moist is her eye!

26

I am the scalp of myself, skinned by my foeman:
Robbed of my strength, he steeped and soaked me,
Dipped me in water, whipped me out again,
Set me in the sun. I soon lost there
The hairs I had had.
                          The hard edge
Of a keen-ground knife cuts me now,
Fingers fold me, and a fowl's pride
Drives its treasure trail across me,
Bounds again over the brown rim,
Sucks the wood-dye, steps again on me,
Makes his black marks.
                          A man then hides me
Between stout shield-boards stretched with hide,
Fits me with gold. There glows on me
The jewelsmith's handiwork held with wires.

   Let these royal enrichments and this red dye
And splendid settings spread the glory
Of the Protector of peoples — and not plague the fool.
If the sons of men will make use of me
They shall be the safer and the surer of victory,
The wiser in soul, the sounder in heart,
The happier in mind. They shall have the more friends,
Loving and kinsmanlike, kind and loyal,
Good ones and true, who will gladly increase
Their honour and happiness, and, heaping upon them
Graces and blessings, in the embraces of love
Will clasp them firmly. Find out how I am called,
My celebrated name, who in myself am holy,
Am of such service, and salutary to men.

27

Men are fond of me. I am found everywhere,
Brought in from the woods and the beetling cliffs,
From down and from dale. In the daylight wings
Raised me aloft, then into a roof's shade
Swung me in sweetly. Sweltered then
By men in a bath, I am a binder now,
Soon a thrasher, a thrower next:
I'll put an old fellow flat on the ground.
A man who tries to take me on,
Tests my strength, soon finds out,
If his silly plan doesn't pall on him,
That it is his back that will hit the dust.
Loud in words, he has lost control
Of his hands and feet, and his head doesn't work:
His strength has gone. Guess my name
Who have such mastery of men on earth
That I knock them about in broad daylight.

28

Part of the earth is prepared fittingly
With what is hardest and what is sharpest
And what is least merciful of what men possess.
Cut down, rubbed out, rolled out, dried out,
Bound and twisted, blanched and sodden,
Decked and dollied, it is drawn from afar
To the doors of men. Mirth is indoors then
Among living creatures, increases and lasts
For as long as it lives. A long while
They have all they want — not a word against it —
But after it is gone they begin to mutter
And speak differently. A difficult matter
For a sagacious man to sound this creature.

29

A curious and wonderful creature I saw,
— bright air-grail, brave artefact —
Homing from a raid with its haul of silver
Brimming precarious crescent horns.
To build itself a hideaway high up in the city,
A room in a tower, timbered with art,
Was all it aimed at, if only it might.

Then over the wall rose a wonder familiar
To the earth-race, to everyone known.
It gathered to itself the hoard, and to its home drove off
That unhappy outcast. Onward it coursed,
Wandered westward with wasting heart.

Dust rose to the skies, dew fell to the earth,
Night was no more. No man knew
Along what ways it wandered after.

30

I am fire-fretted and I flirt with Wind
And my limbs are light-freighted and I am lapped in flame
And I am storm-stacked and I strain to fly
And I am a grove leaf-bearing and a glowing ember.

From hand to friend's hand about the hall I go,
So much do lords and ladies love to kiss me.
When I hold myself high, and the whole company
Bow quiet before me, their blessedness
Shall flourish skyward beneath my fostering shade.

Strange the creature that stole through the water.
Grandly she called from her keel to the land,
Lifted her loud voice. Her laughter was fearful,
Awful where it was known; her edges sharp.
Slow to enter, she was not slack in battle;
Hard, and, in deeds of destruction, unyielding:
She crushed wooden walls. Wicked the spell
That she cunningly unbound about her creation:
'My mother—and I am the most daring
Of all the sex—is also my daughter
When grown up in strength. It is granted likewise
By the wise among the people, that in every part of the earth,
In whatever station, she stands gracefully.'

34

She feeds the cattle, this creature I have seen
In the houses of men. Many are her teeth
And her nose is of service to her. Netherward she goes,
Loyally plundering and pulling home again;
She hunts about the walls in hope of plants,
Finding always some that are not firmly set.
She leaves the fair fast-rooted ones
To stand undisturbed in their established place,
Brightly shining, blossoming and growing.

35

The womb of the wold, wet and cold,
Bore me at first, brought me forth.
I know in my mind my making was not
Through skill with fells or fleeces of wool;
There was no winding of wefts, there is no woof in me,
No thread thrumming under the thrash of strokes,
No whirring shuttle steered through me,
No weaver's reed rapped my sides.
The worms that braid the broidered silk
With Wierd cunning did not weave me;
Yet anywhere over the earth's breadth
Men will attest me a trustworthy garment.

Say truly, supple-minded man,
Wise in words, what my name is.

38

I watched a beast of the weaponed sex.
He forced, fired by the first of lusts,
Four fountains which refreshed his youth
To shoot out shining in their shaped ways.

A man stood by that said to me:
'That beast, living, will break clods;
Torn to tatters, will tie men's hands.'

42

I saw two wonderful and weird creatures
Out in the open unashamedly
Fall a-coupling. If the fit worked,
The proud blonde in her furbelows got
What fills women.
                                    The floor's my table:
The runes I trace tell any man
Acquainted with books both the creatures'
Names in one. Need (N) shall be there
Twice over; Oaks (A) twice;
And the bright Ash (Æ) —one only in the line—
And Hail (H) twice too. Who the hoard's door
With a key's power can unlock
That guards the riddle against rune-guessers,
Holds its heart close, hides it loyally
With cunning bonds? Clear now
To men at wine by what names
This shameless couple are called among us.

43

I know of one who is noble and brave,
A guest in our courts. Neither grim hunger
Nor hot thirst can harm him at all,
Neither age nor illness. If only the servant
Whom on his journey he has to have with him
Serves him faithfully, they shall find appointed,
When safe in their homeland, happiness and feasting,
Untold bliss — but bitterness otherwise,
If the lord's servant serves his master
Ill on the way. One must not be
A burden to his brother or both will suffer
When they are jointly drawn on their journey elsewhere
And must leave the company of the kinswoman who is
Their only sister and their mother. Let the man who will,
Declare graciously how the guest might be called,
Or else the servant, whom I speak of here.

44

Swings by his thigh a thing most magical!
Below the belt, beneath the folds
Of his clothes it hangs, a hole in its front end,
Stiff-set and stout, but swivels about.
Levelling the head of this hanging instrument,
Its wielder hoists his hem above the knee:
It is his will to fill a well-known hole
That it fits fully when at full length.
He has often filled it before. Now he fills it again.

45

I have heard of something hatched in a corner:
It thrusts, rustles, raises its hat.
A bride grabbed at that boneless thing,
Handled it proudly: a prince's daughter
Covered that swelling creature with her robe.

47

I heard of a wonder, of words moth-eaten;
That is a strange thing, I thought, weird
That a man's song be swallowed by a worm,
His binded sentences, his bedside stand-by
Rustled in the night — and the robber-guest
Not one whit the wiser for the words he had mumbı

50

There is on earth a warrior wonderfully engendered:
Between two dumb creatures it is drawn into brightness
For the use of men. Meaning harm, a foe
Bears it against his foe. Fierce in its strength,
A woman may tame it. Well will he heed
And meekly serve both men and women
If they have the trick of tending him,
And feed him properly. He promotes their happiness,
Enhances their lives. Allowed to become
Proud, however, he proves ungrateful.

51

I saw four fine creatures
Travelling in company; their tracks were dark,
Their trail very black. The bird that floats
In the air swoops less swiftly than their leader;
He dived beneath the wave. Drudgery was it
For the fellow that taught all four of them their ways
On their ceaseless visits to the vessel of gold.

52

I saw the captives carried into the barn
Under the hall's roof: a hard pair,
They have been taken and tightly bound
In a firm lashing. Leaning on the second
Was a dark Welsh girl, who directed them,
Cramped in their fetters, on their course together.

53

I saw a tree standing above the wood,
Bright in its branches. It was a blissful tree,
A living piece of wood. Water and earth
Fed it well: until, full of years,
It was transformed in terrible sort.
Dumb it lay, its deep mutilations
Overclenched with iron: and on its front,
Dark adornment. Dire is his proceeding
As he opens a way now with the weight of his head
For another visitant. Their violence joined,
They have plundered many hoards. If, for his partner's sake,
The first has risked some fearful narrow place,
His fellow has followed him fast enough.

54

This knave came in where he knew she'd be,
Standing in a corner. He stepped across to her
With the briskness of youth, and, yanking up his own
Robe with his hands, rammed something stiff
Under her girdle as she stood there,
Did what he wanted; they wobbled about.
The serving-man hurried. His servant was capable,
Useful at times; but at every bout
His strength grew tired sooner than hers did,
Weary of the grind. Gradually there were signs
That there grew beneath her girdle what good men often
Long for in their hearts and lay out good money for.

57

Their dark bodies, dun-coated,
When the breeze bears them up over the backs of the hills
Are black, diminutive. Bold singers,
They go in companies, call out loudly;
They tread the timbered cliff, and at times the eaves
Of men's houses. How do they call themselves?

60

I was by the sand at the sea-wall once:
Where the tide comes I kept my dwelling,
Fast in my first seat. There were few indeed
Of human kind who cared to behold
My homeland in that lonely place,
But in every dawning the dark wave
Lapped about me. Little did I think
That early or late I ever should
Speak across the meadbench, mouthless as I am,
Compose a message. It is a mysterious thing,
Dark to the mind that does not know
How a knife's point and a clever hand,
A man's purpose and a point also,
Have pressed upon me to the purpose that
I might fearlessly announce, for none but us two,
A message to you, so that no man beside
Might spread abroad what is spoken between us.

61

A noble lady used to lock me up
Tight in a box. She took me out sometimes
With her own hands, offered me to her lord,
According to the courteous request of her prince.
Up into my bosom then he would introduce his head,
Fixing it in the narrow part from a netherward direction.
If he who took me was tough enough,
What had to fill me — well furnished as I am —
Would be something rough. Resolve my meaning.

65

Alive, I spoke not: I was not spared for that.
Where I existed, I have persisted. All possess themselves of m
They keep me in restraint, cut off my head,
Bite my bare body, break my growth.
Unless he bit me I bit no man:
Many of them there be that bite me.

66

I am more than this ancient middle-earth,
Less than an itch in the palm, more light than the moon,
Swifter than the sun. The seas and the waters
And the green expanse of the earth's bosom,
All I contain. I touch the depths,
Stoop below hell, overstep the heavens,
The land of glory, look down from afar
On the home of the angels. The earth and what
From of old enfolds it, the ocean's stream,
I fill with myself. Say what I am called.

68

The wave, over the wave, a wierd thing I saw,
Thorough-wrought, and wonderfully ornate:
A wonder on the wave — water became bone.

69

The thing is magic, unimaginable
To him who knows not how it is.
It throstles through its sides, its throat angled
And turned with knowledge, two barrels
Set sharp on the shoulder.
                              Its shaping is fulfilled
As it stands by the wayside so wonderful to see,
Tall and gleaming, to glad the passer-by.

70

I am clad in red, a rich man's treasure.
I was a steep hard place: plants grew on me,
Bright to look at. What's left of me now
Is the work of the fire, the file's anger:
Tightly imprisoned, made precious with wire.
One who wears gold may weep at my bite
When I dash to pieces his precious treasure.

71

Small, I fed myself from four dear brothers,
Tugged at them often. Each of them gave me
To drink every day at different times
Through a small hole. I was happy in my growing up
Until I was of years to yield this task
To the dark herdsman. I went to distant places,
Trod the Welsh marches, trudged the upland
Roped beneath a beam, a ring on my neck.
I endured toil and trouble on that path,
My share of misery. Many times the iron
Sorely pricked my side. Silent was I:
To no man did I ever make complaint
Even when the pricks were painful to me.

72

I stood in the plain, stayed where I was fed
By the earth and the clouds, until, old in years,
I was changed by men who meant me no good.
They took me from home, turned my nature
From the character I had when I held my life,
And contrived that I must, contrary to my growing up,
Bow my will often to the will of a slayer.
Now I am a menace in my master's hand,
A power of evil, if his valour is good
Or he seeks glory. . .

    My sides are yellow, slender is my neck. . .
When the sun of battle shines bright on me.
He tends me with care, keeps me hidden
When he takes me in the troop. Too widely is it known
That among the bold ones I have the brains of a thief. . .
Sometimes I go on and openly break into
A defended place that was formerly quite secure.
He hurries away in haste from that place,
Leaves the city, the soldier who
Knows my nature. Name me.

73

I was a pure girl and a grey-maned woman
And, at the same time, a singular man.
I flew with the birds, breasted the sea,
Sank beneath the wave, dissolved among fish
And alighted on land. I had a living soul.

75

I saw a woman sit alone.

76

I fed in the deep folds of the sea:
Waves covered me, close to the land.
Often to the ocean I opened my mouth:
Foot had I none. Now my flesh will be
Meat for a man. He'll not mind my outside
Once his knife's sharpness has sheared a way
Between me and my hide. Hastily then
He'll eat me, uncooked. . .

79

Hwæt!
I am always at the ætheling's shoulder,
His battle-fellow, bound to him in love,
I follow the king. Flaxen-headed
Lady may lay her light hand on me,
Though she be of clearest blood, an earl's child.
I hold in my heart the hollow tree's fruit,
Ride out in front on a fierce steed
When the host goes harrying, harsh-tongued then,
Bear to songsmith when singing's done
His word-won gift. I have a good nature,
And in myself am swart. Say what I am called.

80

I am puff-breasted, proud-crested,
A head I have, and a high tail,
Eyes and ears and one foot,
Both my sides, a back that's hollow,
A very stout beak, a steeple neck
And a home above men. Harsh are my sufferings
When that which makes the forest tremble takes and shakes me.
Here I stand under streaming rain
And blinding sleet, stoned by hail;
Freezes the frost and falls the snow
On me stuck-bellied. And I stick it all out
For I cannot change the chance that made me.

84

My home is not silent: I myself am not loud.
The Lord has provided for the pair of us
A joint expedition. I am speedier than he
And sometimes stronger; he stays the course better.
Sometimes I rest, but he runs on.
For as long as I live I live in him;
If we leave one another it is I who must die.

85

Many were met, men of discretion
Wisdom and wit, when in there walked. . .

Two ears it had, and one eye solo,
Two feet and twelve hundred heads,
Back, belly, a brace of hands,
A pair of sides and shoulders and arms
And one neck. Name, please.

86

I saw an odd creature, its ample belly
Mightily swollen. The man who attended
Had great strength in his hands. Huge he seemed to me,
A good man for a battle. He grabbed hold of it,
And with heaven's tooth. . .
Blew in its eye. It barked out,
Wagged with a will. . .

90

My head has been beaten upon by a hammer,
Pierced with a spoke, smoothed with a file.
There is a spike opposite I must often swallow
When, ring-stiffened, I strive forward
Hard against what is hard, and, hollowed out behind,
Force backwards the defender of what
Delights my master in the middle of the night.
Sometimes my muzzle makes the warden
Of my lord's treasure retract — when his wish is
To receive the things of those persons
Whose departure from life he has personally arranged.

91

I grew from the ground, bore a glad life;
Among the trees of the forest was preferred by the brown one
Smiling ones came to me; I carried her messages;
Was golden in the courts. Caught in a ring now,
I bring joy to a warrior as a weapon of battle. . .

92

My lord .   .   .   .   .   .
            .   .   .   for his own pleasure
        .   .   .   .   .   .
Lofty *and delightful* .   .   .
        .   .   . *a sharp* .   .   . ; sometimes .   .   .
        .   .   . *sometimes* my lord
Sought .   .   .   .   .   . went
When old in years, over the *deep streams*,
By the steep cliffs he had to climb sometimes
To gain his home, or again descended,
Sought the advantage of the valley floor,
Firm on his feet. In frost the stony plains
Held his traces. The hoary one shook
Rime from his coat then. I rode that swift creature
As his crowning joy, until cast from my place
By my younger brother who usurped my seat.
Afterwards iron inwardly wounded me
With its brown bite; but no blood came,
No gore from my body, though it bit me hard,
The keen-edged steel. I did not cry at that hour
Nor wept for the wound; I could not wreak vengeance
On the life of that warrior for my lamentable fate,
But endured all the dire things
That carved my outside. I catch in my mouth now
Black wood and water; my belly contains
Some dark thing that drops down upon me
As I stand here on my single foot.
Now my hoard is preyed on by a pilfering foe
Who once carried far the comrade of the wolf:
From out of my belly he often goes,
Steps on the hard board .   .   .
        .   .   . *a portion of death*, when the candle of the day,
the sun .   .   .   .   .   .
            .   .   . looks with his eyes on the work,
and .   .   .   .   .   .

Notes

THE TEXTS AND NUMBERING of the riddles adopted here are those of W. S. Mackie in his edition of the Exeter Book, Part II, for the Early English Text Society (Oxford University Press, 1934), but I am also indebted to two other of the older editors: A. J. Wyatt, whose *Old English Riddles* (D. C. Heath, Boston, 1912) has a fine critical introduction, with notes and glossary, and E. V. K. Dobbie, to whose *Anglo-Saxon Poetic Records*, Vol. III, *The Exeter Book* (edited with G. P. Krapp, Columbia University Press, 1936) I also owe a few readings.

The present little book is not intended as a contribution to current scholarship, and the following notes contain only minimal indications. As the Exeter Book has been used as a cutting-board and a beer-mat and has also been damaged by fire, the texts of some riddles, especially towards the end of the book, are defective. Lacunae are indicated (by dots) only where they occur in the middle of the text of a riddle, except in the case of 92, which, as the note explains, is preserved entire as a specimen of the ruinous state of the text.

2   'the Spearman' (line 3): Neptune.

10   A popular piece of natural history.

11   Beer, ale, wine and mead are all possibles. Cf. 27, 28.

12   'Welsh' (line 4): the conquered Britons. Cf. 52. Also 38, 71.

14   Cf. 79, 92.

15   Scholars discuss whether these characteristics best fit what was then believed of badgers, porcupines or hedgehogs.

18   Probably a fragment, of uncertain solution.

25   *Cannabis* has also been proposed. But cf. 65. Wyatt remarks (page xxx) 'The absence of lubricity in Old English poetry is so remarkable, that the breach of the rule in the *double entendre* riddles (nos. 25, 44, 45, 54, 61, 62) leads me to attribute to them a folk origin.'

26   I have for this volume completed the last ten lines of the translation omitted in *The Earliest English Poems*.

27   For the reference to honey in line 5, cf. 79.

30   The final guise of the wood is a Cross. Cf. *The Dream of the Rood*.

35 'Wierd' (line 10) represents the Old English *wyrd*, fate, from which Shakespeare's 'weird sisters' descend. This apparently animistic and sternly Anglo-Saxon riddle is a direct translation of Aldhelm's *De Lorica*.

38 Cf. 71.

42 The runic characters can be read as *hana* and *hæn*, cock and hen.

44 Cf. 90.

47 Cf. 51, 92.

53 Cf. the note to 30 above.

68 A free combination of what may be two riddles.

69 Cf. Vergil, *Eclogues*, vii, 24: *hic arguta sacra pendebit fistula pinu* ('And hang my pipe upon the sacred pine' — Dryden).

73 The riddle has been retranslated in line with the new, convincing (and brilliant) solution proposed by Mr Arthur Cooper in his review in *Agenda* Vol. 19, No. 1.

76 The ending is damaged; a line and a half are missing.

79 *Hwæt!* is the Old English exclamation calling for attention, and often begins a poem. Cf. 87, 92. For solution, cf. 92. Line 6 refers to the honey in the mead. Cf. 27.

80 The last line is damaged, but I follow Mackie.

85 Derived from Symphosius' riddle 95, *Luscus allium vendens*.

91 Cf. 30, 72. The 'brown ones' of line 2 are explained as swine, who ate the beech-mast. In Old English 'beech' is, as well as the tree, the plural of 'book'. This could explain line 3, but the tree could equally have been a trysting-place where messages were left.

92 The first eight and the last five lines are presented exactly as in the facing text of W. S. Mackie, *verbatim*, with the translations of reconstructed words italicized, dots, medial space for the caesura, and all.

70

Suggested Solutions

1	Storm on land	45	Dough
2	Storm at sea	47	Book-worm
3	Earthquake, Storm at sea, Thunderstorm	50	Fire
		51	Handwriting
5	Shield	52	Flail
7	Wild swan	53	Battering-ram
8	Jay or Jackdaw?	54	Churn
9	Cuckoo	57	Swallows
10	Barnacle goose	60	Reed
11	Drink	61	Helmet
12	Ox-hide	65	Onion
14	Horn	66	Nature
15	Badger	68	Ice
16	Anchor	69	Shepherd's pipe
18	Wineskin	70	Iron
25	Onion	71	Ox
26	Gospel Book	72	Spear
27	Mead	73	Snow
28	Barley	75	?
29	Moon and Sun	76	Oyster
30	Wood	79	Horn
33	Iceberg, Ice	80	Weather-cock
34	Rake	84	Fish in river
35	Coat of mail	85	One-eyed Garlic Seller
38	Bullock	86	Bellows
42	Cock and Hen	90	Key
43	Soul and Body	91	Beech, Book
44	Key	92	Antler, Horn inkstand